Money

The Top 100 Best Ways To Make And Manage Money

By Ace McCloud
Copyright © 2014

Disclaimer

The information provided in this book is designed to provide helpful information on the subjects discussed. This book is not meant to be used, nor should it be used, to diagnose or treat any medical condition. For diagnosis or treatment of any medical problem, consult your own physician. The publisher and author are not responsible for any specific health or allergy needs that may require medical supervision and are not liable for any damages or negative consequences from any treatment, action, application or preparation, to any person reading or following the information in this book. Any references included are provided for informational purposes only. Readers should be aware that any websites or links listed in this book may change.

Table of Contents

DEDICATED TO THOSE WHO ARE PLAYING THE GAME OF LIFE TO

WIN

KEEP ON PUSHING AND NEVER GIVE UP!

Ace McCloud

Be sure to check out my website for all my Books and Audio books.

www.AcesEbooks.com

Introduction

I want to thank you and congratulate you for buying the book: Money- The Top 100 Best Ways To Make And Manage Money.

This book will provide you with time tested and proven methods to bring more money into your life. There are things that you can do on a daily basis that will pay huge dividends for your financial wellbeing over the long term. In this book you will also discover some of the biggest mistakes that people make with money and how to avoid them yourself. You will also find out the keys to money management success that the wealthiest people in the world use on a regular basis. If you're not happy with your yearly income and are finally ready to do something about it, then this is the book for you!

Money might be printed on a fancy piece of paper, but its importance in everyday life cannot be denied! However, what you may not know is that money doesn't have to control you—you can learn how to control it. Have you ever lost sleep over not knowing whether your bills were going to get paid? I know I have and it's a horrible feeling. When you master good money-handling habits, eventually all of your financial worries can simply melt away. You don't have to be a Wall Street genius to utilize the strategies in this book. There are many great ways to better manage your money and there are even more ways to generate additional income! The key is to discover which strategies work best for you, and then to implement them intelligently.

Why is it so important to master money? Well, it's true that you can fall into a pretty bad pitfall if you don't—you could lose the roof over your head, the car that gets you to and from work, the electricity that keeps your devices running, and the gas that keeps you warm at night. Although it is important to not let money control your life and you should always be grateful for the things in your life that money *can't* buy, the reality is that money makes the world go round. Money is required to raise children, buy food, purchase clothes, acquire the latest gadgets and so much more that keeps your life going smoothly.

If money is in short supply, it can often lead to mental stress, relationship problems, and a variety of other negative consequences. Mental stress from lack of money can tire you out, wear you down, and make you physically sick. It can take away from your best performances and it can determine whether you keep a job, a relationship and a happy life. Some people let their money problems go unresolved for so long that it ends up entirely consuming everything they have. Unresolved money problems can come back to haunt you in the future, too. They can ruin your credit score and make it harder for you to take out loans and mortgages. Once your credit has gone bad, then it is even more expensive for you to get around in daily life!

By learning how to master the art of handling money, your life can be so much better! You'll never have to worry about late bill payments, emergency medical bills, car maintenance, or anything else that currently seems to suck the hard-earned money right out of your pocket. You'll be able to focus on more important aspects of your life, such as spending time with your family, traveling and exploring new places, enjoying your favorite hobby and anything else you've ever dreamed of! You'll be able to afford the extras and not worry one bit! So get ready to take control of your finances once and for all! Your journey to financial freedom begins here.

Chapter 1: Wiring Your Brain For Financial Success

Before you can even think about earning and saving more money, you have to mentally prepare yourself first. Has anyone ever told you, "it's all in your head?" When it comes to money, that's nearly the truth! Before we dive into the different ways you can save and earn more money, it is crucial that you learn how to handle money in your brain first. Once you have mastered this, you will find it much easier to handle money in real life.

How to Grow Your Income

When it comes to you and your money, it is important to remember that your income can only go as far as you can. Do you know anybody who has ever won the lottery? Studies actually have found that people who have suddenly won or inherited large amounts of money often end up losing it all after several years—and it's likely not a coincidence. In many of these cases, these people did not have what it takes to handle their money, mentally. Interestingly, people who have worked themselves into being millionaires can often incur financial tragedies and still manage to get back on their feet within a short period of time.

Think about it—if you believe that you don't deserve a lot of money, will you be successful in handling it? If you have a shopping addiction and you do nothing to overcome it, what will your wallet look like? Does your character reflect your income? The point is that your financial situation will often reflect who you are as a person—the more successful you are in personal growth, the more your earning potential can be. If you're the type of person who has the ability to exert willpower and discipline when it comes to kicking bad habits, going after goals, and being honest with yourself about your finances, chances are you'll be much more well-off financially.

They key to setting yourself up for financial success is to start from within. It is very easy to dream of becoming a millionaire, living in a mansion, and driving behind the wheel of a brand new car—but first, you must prepare yourself to get all of those things. Money doesn't grow on trees but it does grow from desire and ambition. Think back to school when you learned about cause and effect—there is an effect for every cause—your weight is an effect of what you eat, your knowledge is an effect of your desire to learn, and your money is an effect of what you do to earn and manage it.

I have a story to share that can help you gain a better perspective on this. My friend once worked in the quick service restaurant industry as a manager. One thing that she noticed among most of her workers was that they were not happy about their pay. They would often complain about not getting raises or not getting enough hours but she began to notice a pattern. The same people who complained never sought to do anything about their complaints. They would just do the bare minimum requirements of their job and then go home. They never looked to go above and beyond to prove to their upper management that they were worthy of what they felt they deserved. Even when they had dreams of being successful in other areas of employment, they would never take the effort or initiative to go after those dreams, even when encouraged to do so.

What set my friend aside from her co-workers was that she had the determination and persistence that it took to move up the financial ladder—to get into management, she didn't even wait for the offer—she went out and became certified on her own to give herself an edge. Then, eventually, she wasn't happy about her income at the restaurant either and decided that she deserved more than what she was getting. So, she went out, bought some business books, and launched her own business, finally able to break the roof that was blocking her earning potential and she was finally able to leave the restaurant industry. It didn't even take a degree in business for her to do that.

The moral of the story is that you are the only person who can change the way your money comes to you and stays with you. The great news is that *anyone* can learn how to wire their brains for ultimate financial success. All it takes is a couple of small, simple changes that you can easily implement into your life by making them habits.

Review Your Emotions. Your emotions can be one of the most influential factors that determine where you go in life. As many experts have theorized, your thoughts lead to feelings, your feelings lead to actions, and your actions lead to results. The key is to understand what is driving your feelings, as your feelings are what start the chain of results. The way your emotions are toward money can be very influencing over how you end up handling it. Think about how money was viewed in your household while you were growing up—did you ever hear your parents or guardians say things such as, "money is the root of all evil" or "rich people are stingy, greedy people who aren't like us?" If you grew up hearing those things in person or on TV, than there is a good chance that you are letting your emotions take charge of your finances as an adult. Luckily, there are ways to change your emotions toward money.

Special Exercise—Take out a notebook and write down your thoughts on how you and your family viewed money while you were growing up. Just try to get out any negative things that you heard about it. This will help you raise your awareness about your emotions toward money. Once you've done that, write down your thoughts on how those beliefs may have influenced the way you view money now. One helpful thing you can do is say something out loud to counter those beliefs. For example, if you grew up hearing that "Money is the root of all evil," tell yourself, "Having more money allows me to do more good in the world." You can also do quick positive affirmations whenever your mind may be going negative or anytime you want to start building a solid wealth foundation in your mind. Some examples of positive wealth building affirmations are: "Money comes to me quickly and easily." Or "I am a money magnet." Go ahead and make up your own affirmation and repeat it to yourself regularly. One of my favorite times to do this is on my daily walk.

Review Your Financial Habits. Your habits are the second biggest factor in influencing how you manage your money. <u>Habits</u> are things that you do automatically, so if you have bad financial habits, chances are your money management is poor. For example, if you just always have to buy something when you go to the store, you'll have to break that habit to avoid spending more money than you should, especially if you could be getting a better deal online or somewhere else. If you're used to living off other people, that is definitely a habit that you should break because one day, you might wind up on your own, and you will probably have no idea how to handle money wisely. On the other hand, if you can resist buying something every time you go to a store or if you are working toward becoming financially independent by furthering your knowledge, searching for higher-paying jobs, etc, then you will have some great habits and your money-handling skills will tend to be greater.

Special Exercise—Think and write about your bad habits concerning money. Do you tend to ignore your bank statements? Are you often late on your bill payments? Do you carry cash, cards, or both and how does that impact your spending? Do you have a savings account? Do you spend a lot of money on things that you know are unhealthy? Try to think of the bad habits that will affect you the most negatively in the future. Next, carefully consider each one and ask yourself out loud how that habit has adversely affected your wallet. From each bad habit, analyze the consequences and learn from your mistake. Tell yourself out loud, "I can and I will change my bad money-handling habits." Be 100% honest with yourself, as nobody will know about these thoughts except for you.

Review Your Specific Beliefs About Money. Finally, you must dig deep and grasp the roots of what is causing your most specific, emotional belief about money. When you were little, what do remember experiencing that concerned money? Many people grow up believing false assumptions, such as "men are the breadwinners," or "women are meant to stay home and take care of the house," or "money is what makes people get divorced," etc. Whatever assumptions and specific emotional memories you have of money can seriously influence the way you handle it.

Special Exercise: Think about the most significant emotional memory you have had concerning money and write about how it may have impacted your life today. Then, say something out loud to try and distance yourself from that memory. Saying something along the lines of, "I will not let this memory affect how I handle money today."

Wire Your Brain Continuously. Once you have consciously made the decision to distance yourself from your previous beliefs about money, the next step is to wire your brain to start handling money better. Think about what you're making now and how you're spending it. Can you do better? Are you struggling to pay your bills? Answering all of these questions is very important for properly reprogramming your brain to handle money. Once you have answered those questions it's time to start using positive affirmations to combat your old negative thinking behavior. You also want to program your brain for financial abundance. So you can visualize money coming to you in all sorts of different ways and you could also try to think of one hundred dollar bills as one dollar bills to help program your brain for financial abundance. I would also highly recommend Hypnosis for those who are serious about programming their brain for financial success. My favorite source for great audios is hypnosis downloads. I personally use and can highly recommend "The Millionaire Mindset" bundle package or you can try: "Overcome Fear of Money."

 If you really want to go to the next level of brain mind technology and program positive associations of money into your brain, than I would also recommend subliminal messaging. There is a great program that I use on my computer every day called Subliminal Power. This program is super easy to use and it allows you to custom make your own subliminal messages. Another great feature is that you can add pictures to the subliminal messages and the program comes with some great brainwave music as well.

How to Set Financial Goals

Once you have mentally prepared yourself for financial success, the next step is to set your goals and get to work on them. When setting financial goals, it is important to set short-term, mid-term, and long-term goals. For example, a short-term financial goal could be to pay off the last remaining balance of your car loan. An example of a mid-term goal could be to have three thousand dollars in a bank account for use in emergencies. An example of a long-term goal could be to have all your debt paid off in three years.

A great way to stick to your goals is to have a visual chart. Here is a worksheet that you can easily copy down on a piece of paper to help yourself get started and organized:

	Target Completion Date	~Total Cost	Amount Saved	Amount Needed to Finish
Short-Term Goal				
Mid-Term Goal				
Long-Term Goal				

Next, think about any time in the past where you have set financial goals. Did you achieve them or did you utterly fail? If you failed, think about why that happened and learn from your mistake so that you won't make it again today.

After that, ask yourself the famous question, "**what motivates you?**" If you're not motivated by anything to start changing your financial habits, then you probably will not succeed. Really sit down and think about this question for a while. Many people are motivated to improve their money management skills so they can take more vacations, attract a new love interest, buy a new house or car, buy a boat, send their children to private school or college, or have enough money to take care of a parent later in life. Those are just a few common examples, your motivation may be entirely different, and that's okay! Just make absolutely sure to not skip this step until you have a clear idea in your mind as to why you are going to do the things you do in order to be financially free.

Finally, review your goal chart and make sure that your goals are challenging yet realistic. Don't set goals that are too easy and don't set goals that are impossible to reach. Make sure they are logical, easy to track, realistic, and important to you. A great strategy to start off each goal with the phrase: "I will easily..."

If you really want to do your goals like a professional, then I would highly recommend the Goals On Track program. It is by far the best goal setting program that I have ever come across! It e-mails your goals to you daily for easy reference, it allows you to attach pictures to your goals, easily tracks goal progress and the program also comes with a vision board and journal.

Once you have made your goals, it is time to start going out there and getting them accomplished! But wait—there's more to rewiring your brain when it comes to money management...

Prepare a Budget

Preparing your own personalized budget is important so that you can become aware of just how much money you're spending each month and how much money you will need to save. Many people turn to professional financial advisers but you can easily make your own perfect budget right here in this chapter. All it takes is a few easy steps:

1) **Save Copies of Every Bill You Pay and Take Them Out.** Gather up everything that costs you money each month—rental payment receipts, utility bills, loan payments receipts, and your bank statements. Don't forget to count all expenses like grocery shopping, gas for your car, entertainment, etc. To ensure that you can best keep track of your money, a good idea is to rarely carry cash with you and to pay everything with a debit or credit card—that way, all of your purchases can be tracked onto your bank statement. That idea is totally up to you, as many people have different preferences about methods of payment.

2) **Figure Out Where Your Income is Coming From.** Next, take out your pay stubs or make an approximate calculation of how much money you actually bring home each month. Count anything from rental income, self-employment money, or anything else that brings money *into* your pocket. Try to be as accurate as possible.

3) **Divide Expenses Into Two Categories.** Next, organize your bills and expenses and allocate them into one of two categories—fixed or variable. You would put expenses that stay the same, such as your rent or your cable bill in the "fixed" category while you would put expenses that can differ from month-to-month, such as dining out expenses, into the "variable" category. This will be helpful in allowing you to make any necessary changes to your budget later on.

4) **Add It All Together.** Now, add up your monthly expenses and compare it to your total monthly income. If your income is more than your expenses, then you're in pretty good shape and you have the freedom to decide whether you need to make any changes to save more. If your expenses are more than your income then you should definitely look and see where you can make some cuts.

5) **Review.** Finally, it is important to review your budget each month as it can be very easy for your bills to fluctuate. For example, your gas bill may be higher in the winter because you will need to use more heat but your electric bill may go down in the summer if you like to spend a lot of time outdoors. By giving yourself a heads up on what your bills are going to look like for the month, you can make smarter spending decisions.

Make Your Own Definition of Money and Its Purpose. The last step in rewiring your brain to look at money differently is to make up your own definition of money. You know what money is, obviously, but what is it to you? How does money serve you? The answer to this question will be different for everyone but when you're answering it, be completely honest with yourself. Nobody but you will know the answer and you don't have to share it with anybody. Use this answer to motivate yourself towards your financial goals.

Chapter 2: The Top 25 Best Wealthy Habits

During the year 2013, there were 31,680,000 millionaires in the world and 1,426 billionaires. New York City alone is home to 389,000 millionaires. How did these people become millionaires in the first place? While many people have the misconception that millionaires just "got lucky," that's actually very far from the truth. The fact is that many millionaires are self-made and they get there by implementing some very important habits in their lives. Being rich is more like a state of mind than a status. Now, I cannot promise you that by following these habits that you will become a millionaire yourself. There are many other factors that determine how you rise to the top. However, this chapter will take a look at 25 of the most important habits you can form to make the most out your personal money management skills—and who knows...maybe you'll become a millionaire one day, too!

Note: In this next section, rich/wealthy people are those who make an average of over $100,000 a year and poor people are those who make $35,000 or less a year.

Value Good Habits. Over 50% of rich people believe that their daily habits are what attribute the most to their financial security. Try to practice only the best habits that will drive you far in life! For a complete list of great habits that you can develop as well as information on how to break bad habits and make room for new ones, I invite you to also check out my best seller, The Top 100 Best Habits.

Watch What You Eat. Rich people are more likely to eat less junk food a day verses the poor. If you would like to rethink your diet in an attempt to better manage your money, you can find all of the information you need about health and nutrition plus more in some of my other health related books. For this topic, I recommend checking out Ultimate Health Secrets, Ultimate Energy, and Vegetarian Diet, Recipes, and Cooking.

Watch How Often You Gamble. Gambling is a fun way to try and double your money with no work. However, what many people forget is that the odds of winning are often stacked against you. Interestingly, wealthy people are far less likely to gamble than poor people. When I see all these fabulous casinos around the world, it seems pretty obvious to me who the winners truly are.

Set Goals. Did you know that 80% of wealthy people spend their time focusing on one goal at a time? On the other hand, only 12% of poor people are focused on setting goals and achieving them one at a time. Goal-setting is a great way to move yourself from point A to point B in the quickest time possible.

Listen to Audio Programs. More than half of successful rich people listen to audio programs instead of their car radio when driving. Listening to an audio tape while you drive is a great way to squeeze in some extra knowledge effectively. If you don't have enough time to read books, you can consider doing this.

Read. People who spend 30 minutes or more reading non-fiction to further their knowledge and education are 80% more likely to be wealthy.

Practice Cardio. What does your exercise regime look like? Over half of successful wealthy people practice cardio during the week. Less than 30% of poor people find the time to schedule it in.

Organize Yourself. Do you keep a daily to-do list? If you do, then you have the potential to end up among the 81% of people who become wealthy. If you don't, your chances of falling among the 19% of poor people can increase. To-do lists are a powerful yet simple way to organize your life, prioritize your goals, and stay focused on where you're going. My favorite strategy is to cut up computer paper into a bunch of squares. I will then write down all the things that I want to get accomplished. I then put the most important things first and focus all my attention on it until it has been accomplished. I then throw the piece of paper away and move onto the next thing. Also, if priorities change, then it is easy enough to switch the papers around.

Remember Birthdays. Research has found that 80% of people who are wealthy call their friends and family to wish them a Happy Birthday verses only 11% of poor people.

Stay Humble and Modest. Another interesting habit that can determine your level of wealth is whether or not you speak your mind. While only 6% of rich people admit to freely speaking their mind, 69% of poor people do. Granted that you should always stand up for yourself, this statistic focuses more on jumping to conclusions and saying things without first thinking them through.

Network, Network, Network. Networking is a powerful way to climb up the ladder in your career. Research shows that 79% of rich people spend at least five hours a week networking while only 16% of poor people do the same.

Limit Your TV Time. Watching TV is a fun way to pass the time but it is important to monitor and limit how much time you're actually spending on it. Research shows that wealthy people are more likely to only watch one hour of television per day and only 6% have admitted to watching reality shows. On the contrary, approximately 75% of poor people watch more than one hour of TV a day and 78% watch reality shows.

Wake Up Early. Waking up early can help you become so much more productive. It allows you time to work out, eat breakfast, do affirmations and other important things before you actually have to get to work. Rich people tend to wake up much earlier than poor people.

Continuously Improve Yourself. When it comes to self-improvement, you can never work on yourself enough. Research shows that almost 100% of wealthy people believe in continuous self-improvement. It's a great way to live your life and it can really have an impact on your earning potential. You should always be looking for ways to improve yourself and your life.

Go Above and Beyond. 81% of rich people would agree that their wealth is a result of going above and beyond the requirements of their job. On the other side, only 17% of poor people would agree with this point. Additionally, 86% of rich people work an average of 50 hours a week and are happy with their work situation.

Don't Forget to Floss. Another interesting habit of rich people is that they floss their teeth regularly. Research shows that 62% of rich people verses 16% of poor people floss their teeth every day.

Have Faith in the American Dream. Have you ever heard people say, "The American Dream is dead?" I know I've heard it. However, research shows that 87% of wealthy people believe that the American Dream still exists. Never give up on your dreams and keep pursuing them until you're there! Some of the most famous people throughout all of history have had to overcome tremendous obstacles and pick themselves up time and time again before they finally reached their great success.

Value Your Relationships. Valuing your relationships, both on a personal and professional level, can have a great impact on your financial habits. Successful wealthy people understand the power of making their clients feel special by calling them out of the blue just to say hello rather than trying to sell them something.

Meet New People. Making an effort to meet new people can be very powerful. 68% of rich people believe in this while only 11% of poor people do.

Save. Nearly 100% of rich people believe in the power of saving money in addition to earning it. Only 52% of poor people believe in this. Saving money is hugely important, especially if you ever need money to fall back on in the case of an emergency. You should try and save ten percent of your income and put that into a savings account.

Take Control of Your Life. Are you the type of person who believes that there is another force that is driving your life? While only 10% of wealthy people believe in "fate," a whopping 90% of poor people do! While believing in fate may be an important part of your spirituality, it is important to remember that only you can determine how your life will turn out.

Be Creative. 75% of wealthy people believe that creativity is key to becoming financially successful. Only 11% of poor people share this belief. While intelligence is an important factor in what determines your earnings, many companies and businesses rely on creative individuals to help them drive their organizations further. That can only mean that creative people have the potential to earn more money. To learn more about how to tap in to your inner creative genius, feel free to check out my book on Creativity.

Take Risks. Taking risks can be scary but they can also determine how much money you can make. 63% of rich people agree that taking risks can make you much wealthier. If you agree with this also but you're not sure how to become comfortable with risk-taking, you can learn how to conquer that fear in my latest book: Overcome Fear. Taking calculated risks is one of the key factors that has attributed to the creation of many millionaires and wealthy people throughout the world.

Value Time over Money. Time differs from money in the sense that you can't get it back. You can always make money but you can never get a second of your time back once it's been spent. Rich people understand this principle and often manage it by working for themselves and leveraging others to help them. When you are an hourly or salary employee, time often puts a restraint on your earning potential. The only way around this is to learn how to better manage your time on the job to get more done or to consider working for yourself one day.

Never Settle For Less. This point doesn't have a statistic but it speaks for itself. People who earn more money never settle for less. They work with the mindset that there is something out there that is better for them. To financially successful people, there is no ceiling to their earning potential. If you find yourself often times doubting yourself or your abilities, be sure to check out my book on Confidence to help give yourself the self-confidence boost needed for true success.

Chapter 3: Making Money With a Successful Business

Being able to work for yourself is one of the greatest ways to make money because you determine your hours, your workload, your work environment and your pay rate. Most importantly, working for yourself means that there is no limit on your earning potential—if you want to make $1,000 in a week, you can do it without having to worry about your hours getting cut, not getting tips, getting sick, or anything else that may constrain you in a traditional workplace setting. However, making money isn't *that* easy and it requires a great deal of time, commitment, and creativity. This chapter will take a look at what you can do to become a successful business owner so that you can make as much money as you want. Remember; don't get discouraged—you can do it! Hewlett-Packard started up in a garage and Facebook started in a dorm room!

Before we begin, I want you to ask yourself some crucial questions to make sure that you're ready to make this commitment to yourself:

- Are you willing to quit your day job?
- If you want to start with a part-time business for more security, are you willing to make extra time to focus on your business as well as your day job?
- Do you have a means to fund your business?
- Do you have an original idea that will help people?

If those questions sound good to you, then you may have the potential to become a successful business owner. In the next few chapters, you will learn about some great ideas that you can morph into a business of your own, but for now, let's just focus on logistics. The first step to getting there is to create a business plan. It doesn't have to be anything fancy, but a business plan should serve as your guide, especially in the event that your business just takes off very quickly. A business loan can also be helpful if you need some startup money.

How to Write a Business Plan

You can find lots of business plan templates online but you can just as easily start with a blank word document.

On the first page, write your **executive summary.** While you should write this section last, it is a good idea to dedicate a page to it as you begin. This will include your mission statement, general company information, information about your products or services, and your future goals. If you're looking for funding, include any information about potential banks and investors.

On the next page, write your **company description.** In this section, you will get to write more about your company and how it will fulfill the needs of your audience. Write about how exactly your products/services will do that. Here, you can also explain what makes your company unique and how you think it will be successful.

After that, create your **market analysis** page. This section gives you the opportunity to describe the size and scope of your industry as well as your competition. You should also describe your target market audience, which I will explain more about in a bit. If applicable, state how much market share you believe your company can gain and finally, discuss your pricing and pricing strategy. If applicable, describe all of these things for your competition as well.

Next, you can write your section on **organization and management.** In these pages, describe your business structure (I highly recommend that all start-ups begin as a sole proprietorship or a single-member LLC—you can always switch later). Once you've defined your structure, write about the ownership information of your company, including who owns it, who gets what percentage, forms of ownership, etc. Write out a detailed profile about each owner, including details on their educational background and past experience.

In the next section, dedicate a page to describing your **line of product(s) or services.** Here, you can describe what you are offering, how it can benefit your customers, and anything else that applies. Talk about the lifespan of your offering(s) and whether you are financing any research and development work toward future products/services. If you have any patents, trademarks, or copyrights, include the details about them here.

After that, it is time to write about your **marketing and sales strategy.** This section can include information on how you intend to break into your market, how you intend to grow your market share, and how you intend to reach your target market. Talk about the channels you intend to use, such as print ads or radio ads among many other strategies. Discuss how your products/services will get "out there." For example, will your products be available at major retail stores or just online? If you plan to recruit representatives, include the details here. Finally, leave a space where you can track, monitor, and adjust your sales activities. That way, you won't waste too much time knowing whether one strategy is working or not.

If needed, make the next section your **funding request** section. Here, you can discuss how much money you need to get started as well as projecting your future funding needs, where the funds will go specifically and the plans for financial emergencies in the future. Be very specific in planning this out and be sure to include realistic dates and time-frames.

Finally, your last section should be where you state your **financial projections.** This will help any creditors or investors see that you are committed to your business and that it has the potential to make money. Be certain that your financial projections match any amount of funding that you request.

Optionally, you may add an **appendix** at the end that includes anything else relevant to your business (reference letters, resumes, graphs, credit history, etc).

Define Your Target Market Audience

Once your business plan is in the works, it is important to define your target market audience. You might think that your products/services can help everybody and anybody, but the truth is that unless you identify a specific niche, you probably won't be very successful. It is too much to target everyone in the world—everybody is so different and unique. By having a target market audience, you can identify common factors and use those to reel people in.

The key to defining your target market audience is to be specific. Saying that you're going to target "everyone" or "students" or "stay-at-home moms," is way too general. A better example of a target audience would be, "male students, 21-39 years old with a yearly income of less than $40,000 in Central New Jersey."

Of course, it is hard to just come up with a specific niche to market to, but luckily, there are several ways to get started down the right path.

- **Scope Out Your Current Clients.** Are you already doing some form of business, even if it's informal and unofficial? Your target market audience might already be right in front of your eyes—can you identify a pattern among your current clients? Do you serve more men than women or vice versa? Are your clients from in-state or do they all seem to come from Southern California? Are the majority of your clients lawyers? The possibilities are endless. One great way to find a pattern among your clients is to make small profiles for each one and compare them.

- **Scope Out Your Competition.** Don't be a stranger to your competition. Look at their target audience and see if you can find any gaps. It is important to remember that while your competition may be more advanced than you, they don't always know everything. For example, Burger King made a huge change to its target market audience in 2009, when it decided to shift its focus from non-married, middle aged-men to families. If their competition was able to see that, they could have easily came and swallowed up that market before Burger King could.

- **Scope Out Your Product/Service.** Sometimes, the answer is in your product itself. Say you've invented a coffee-machine that also has a built-in cigarette dispenser. Who would this product benefit? Obviously not children and the elderly, but maybe middle-aged adults who don't live in close range of a convenience store that sells cigarettes. On the other hand, say you are a freelance writer who specializes in resumes—you might target rising college freshmen or graduate students who need help selling themselves to another school.

Important Factors to Note:

Ultimately, however you figure out your target market audience, you will need to make sure you've covered all of their details. Take note of age, gender, location, education level, yearly income, occupation, ethnic background, and/or marital status. Also consider the personalities, values, attitudes, behaviors, lifestyles, and/or interests of your target market audience.

Wait, there's more!

Once you've decided on your target market audience, ask yourself these essential questions before you start to market anything:

- Is my audience big enough?
- Will my product/service truly fulfill a need for my audience?
- Do I understand the psychology of my audience?
- Is my product or service affordable to my audience?
- How accessible is my audience?

Build a Team

The next step in launching a successful business is to build a team or at least know what kind of team you'll build in the future. If you want to start out small, by all means, handle everything yourself. However, if your company grows and you are the person behind driving your product or service, you will want to spend more time doing what you do best. In that case, you would probably hire people to handle your marketing, accounting, public relations, etc.

When you first start out, you should have a couple of mentors who are willing to help you go in the right direction. If possible, talk to a few people who are good with money, talk to some investors, talk to people who are already in your field, and definitely talk to an accountant. As a business owner, you will be responsible for filing and paying the taxes owed on your business income, so it is important to get it right the first time to avoid any costly mistakes. Finally, you should definitely talk to a lawyer to see if your company will need anything special. If you are selling products, you will likely need to form a limited liability company (LLC) so that anyone who may sue you cannot go after your personal assets.

Launch!

Once you have completed all these steps, it is time to officially launch. Most businesses are required to file certificates of formations with the state they are in. You can usually find specific information on your home state's Department of Revenue or Department of Treasury website. If you're going to do business under a different name (for example Danny Smith calls his company Just Paintbrushes) you will have to trademark your business name and file additional certificates at a local level. It's also important to note that in some businesses you can file for an LLC in a different state. There can be a lot of advantages to doing this, and the most popular states for forming LLC's in are Nevada, Delaware, and Wyoming. Once you've gotten all of the legalities out of the way, you can go out there and start changing the world!

Chapter 4: Great Business Ideas and Side-Income Gigs

In this chapter, you will learn about the many different ways to make money! You can easily turn any of these ideas into a business with your own spin. Remember to be creative, determined, and never give up on what you want! If any of these ideas catch your eye, be sure to go back to Chapter 3 and set up a business plan for ultimate success!

Business Ideas

Start a DJ Business. Do you have a huge music collection and good tastes? If so, you can consider becoming a DJ. The demand for DJ's is high for weddings, school dances, and local bars/clubs. One night of work could easily net you at least $250-300, depending on your experience and location.

Start a Pallet Furniture Business. If you've ever spent time on social media, you've probably seen ideas for pallet furniture—essentially, furniture made out of pallets. Best of all, many people just *give* wooden pallets away for free! Check Craigslist for the best results. If you have great carpentry and creative skills, you may very well be successful at taking wooden pallets, turning them into furniture, and flipping for a great profit.

Start a House Cleaning Service. If you've got an eye for cleaning and organizing, you could make some really good money cleaning houses on the side. If you do a good job, you could get a lot of repeat customers in this line of business.

Start a Hauling Service. If you own a huge truck, there might be a great way for you to find funding for all the gas it uses up—start a "haul away" service. Many people have big things such as old furniture, scrap-wood, metal, etc. That they need to be taken away and many people don't have access to large trucks.

Be a Rideshare Business. If you do a lot of traveling, you could easily find people who will pay you to take them along and drop them off at your destination or somewhere along the way. You can usually find rideshare requests on Craigslist. Just be sure to use extreme caution when selecting people as your passengers, especially if you are driving alone.

Become a Notary. A notary is valuable for officially binding agreements, documents, and contracts, especially among doctors, lawyers, and real estate agents. You can become certified by taking a course in your state.

Create an Elderly Service Business. If you live in an area that has a high retirement population, you might be able to make really good money doing odd jobs for those who can no longer perform them themselves. Various ideas include shoveling snow, driving them to and from doctor's appointments, helping them go grocery shopping, or helping them fix up their house. Many older people can also get very lonely and would enjoy your company.

Detail Cars. Believe it or not, some people hate washing their own cars or taking them through traditional car washes. If you're willing to get down and dirty, one great idea is to start a home-service car detailing/washing business. It may not bring in *that* much money but you can easily charge $20-25 to wash someone's car for them.

Walk Dogs/Pet Sit. If you love animals, why not help out other people by offering to assist in pet care. Many people with pets work during the day or go on vacation and need somebody to take care of their animals. Your market may be especially good if you live in the city, where many people *need* to walk their dogs for exercise.

Sell Your Baked Goods. If you have a knack for making mouth-watering baked goods, turn it into a business! Sell them at your local bakeries, schools, farmers market, garage sales, community events, and anywhere else you can think of. Many events like to supply food to their attendees and baked goods are usually high on the list.

Start a Merchandising Business. Many big-name companies hire private merchandisers to visit their stores and tend to their big displays. Common things that merchandisers do are water plants, stock shelves, arrange displays, and more. You can easily start your own merchandising service by establishing yourself and then reaching out to several local companies. Work your way up with experience and one day you might be able to reach out to companies like Walmart or Target.

Become a Virtual Assistant. If you're really great at administrative duties and organization, why not consider becoming a virtual assistant? Many people look to outsource work for bookkeeping, research, data entry, email management, website design, correspondence, and a myriad of other things.

Start a Room Renting Business. If you have an extra room in your house or an extra piece of property, don't let it go to waste—rent it out when you can. You can target travelers, students, or families who are looking for a permanent place to live. All the meanwhile, you barely have to move a muscle to earn the rent money.

Set Up a Roadside Stand. If you live in a town that doesn't have a close proximity to restaurants or stores, or if you know a long stretch of road in the middle of nowhere, you can make some extra bucks by setting up a roadside concession stand. Many people who do this sell things such as water, sodas, sports drinks, pretzels, hot dogs, or burgers. You can usually find these products for cheap and then resell them for a profit. If you're in the middle of nowhere, people will likely be more willing to pay a higher price.

Start a Babysitting/Daycare Service. If you are the type of person who is just naturally great with kids, the money might be in it for you with a babysitting or daycare service. Lots of parents don't like to leave their kids with just anybody, so if you can establish yourself as a certified, safe, and highly-rated nanny, you might be able to take the babysitting industry by storm while doing something you love.

Start a Lawn Care Business. It may sound like a "teenage" thing but you can make some great money by mowing and maintaining lawns during the summer. People may be more willing to pay individuals rather than big landscaping companies.

Start a Hair/Make-Up Artist Business. How skilled are you at doing hair and/or make-up? You may be great at it while others can't master it for their life. If you're really talented in that area, try to start a hair/make-up business. A really good target market for this would be girls who are getting ready for their proms, graduations, and/or weddings.

Do Custom Art. If you're a really good artist, you might be able to make money doing caricatures or other artistic self-portraits at community events, weddings, and parties. A good way to get stared is to advertise your services online.

Teach Music. If you grew up mastering an instrument, why not offer to teach other people how to play it? Reading music can be challenging but if you're a great teacher, you can make extra money by sharing your expertise with others who want to learn.

Deliver Newspapers, Phone Books, Etc. If you are willing to take up a route in which you deliver paper products from door to door, you can easily make a nice little side-income each month. Check with your local companies as well as online. Many job boards have delivery opportunities for local areas.

Tutor. If you're a college student or someone who got a great score on your standardized tests, you can make good money tutoring younger students. Many parents believe in a good education and are willing to pay money for their kids to get good grades.

Start an Online Transcription Business. If you have transcribing experience, there are many websites that hire people to do transcriptions. Many sites pay hourly plus bonuses and you can do it right from your home office or living room couch.

Be a Home Staging Person. If you're really good at organization and home decorating, start a home-staging business. That means you help people who are looking to sell their house set it up in a way that would entice others to buy it.

Be a Sales Representative. If you're really good at selling things and networking with people, being a direct sales representative can be a lucrative side business. You can sell anything from home goods to makeup to handbags to candles, as there are many companies who recruit sales reps every day. Some common companies that do this are Pampered Chef and Avon.

Extra Money Ideas

Be a Street Performer. If you have a great talent for playing an instrument, dancing, or doing anything else entertaining, you could set up shop on the street and take money for performances. Just be sure to check with your town about any permits/licenses you may need. Still, it could be a fun way to make money in your spare time.

Help Out Non-Profit Organizations. Often times, non-profit organizations need help with odd jobs such as handing out fliers or putting together mailers. Though they are NPOs, they will usually pay people who are willing to help out. As an added bonus, you'd get to work for an organization that you personally believe in.

Sell Old Electronics. In today's world, it seems like companies are coming out with new electronics almost on the daily. One way to keep your cash flow coming in is to sell your old electronics to people who are still waiting to get older versions. There are many great organizations that allow you to do this.

Help Out at Birthday Parties. If your entertaining skills are high, you might be able to make money helping out at kids' birthdays. You can get paid a decent amount of money to dress up as a character or be in charge of dress-up/face painting.

Share Advice on Your Expertise. Do you have an interesting background in a certain field or industry? If so, you may be able to charge clients to receive valuable advice and guidance. Many industries rely on consultants each year so it's definitely a high-demand area. You also don't need an official degree to do this in most cases. You can even become a life coach, which has become extremely popular recently and something that I may do in the future. In many cases you can do this by e-mail, over the phone, on the Internet, or on Skype.

Get Paid to Watch Sports. If you're a sports-lover, you might be able to score gigs acting as an umpire or referee for your local sport teams, both children and adult leagues. As an added benefit, you'll also get to be part of the action.

Design and Sell T-Shirts. If you're really good at making graphics, you may be able to put them on shirts to sell. You can do this online with websites such as CafePress or Zazzle. If you can design a really funny t-shirt, you can easily make a great profit! A bonus to doing this online is that you won't have to worry about shipping anything out.

Rent Your Parking Space. If you own a condo or home that you don't use year-round, offer to rent out your parking spot for a fee. This works great in tourist areas where it's hard to find a parking spot. Many people will pay a little extra to get a spot nearby the ocean, amusement parks, casinos, etc.

Teach Others. If you have a certain expertise in a subject, put it to good use and teach others! You don't need to have a teaching degree. There are many places online where you can get paid to teach others. Udemy is a good website to explore as well as Skillshare.

Teach a SAT prep course. If you aced the SAT, LSAT, or any other common standardized test, you may be able to make extra money teaching prep courses to those who are getting ready to take the test themselves. Check with your local schools about the demand for prep-courses and make them an offer.

Teach a Special Interest Class. Even if you don't have the best educational knowledge, you can still make money teaching as a special interest teacher. If you're good at dancing, hold dance classes. If you're great at pottery, hold some pottery classes. Many local community centers will allow you to hold a class there and it can net some good money. If you charge $25 a head and you teach a class of 10 people, that's $250 right there.

Sell Your Notes. If you've taken a class and you no longer need your notes and materials, you can sell them to incoming students. There are many places online where you can sell your notes to other students and some colleges even have their own location where you can do this. If you earned an A, earn some money off it, too!

Teach Swimming Lessons. Are you a great swimmer? If so, see if you can become a swimming instructor. Many parents like to teach their kids to swim as early as possible.

Be a Mystery Shopper. Do you love to shop and pay attention to detail? If so, you could take on the role of being a mystery shopper. Many companies will pay you to shop at their business and write a detailed report telling of your experience.

Be a Car Test Driver. Do you love to drive cars? You can actually get paid to do so! Many dealers will pay you at least $25 for you to give your feedback about a new car. They also use it as an incentive to get you to buy the actual car.

Donate Bodily Items. If you are in good health you may be able to help another person out and get paid good money to donate your eggs, sperm, hair, plasma, or any other bodily fluid that is in demand.

Recycle. This may not bring in a huge amount of money, but if you collect aluminum cans and recycle them you can get a few cents per can depending on where you're located, and you will be also doing your good deed for the environment. Although I once heard of a woman who actually made $73,000 from recycling full time!

Write Greeting Cards. If you're really coming up with short punchlines or catchy sentences, you may be able to put them in greeting cards. Check around online for companies who allow you to submit your ideas.

Write Articles. Do you ever wonder where the information you read on places like About.com or ehow.com come from? It actually comes from freelance writers. Many online sites such as Yahoo Contributor and Examiner.com pay writers a flat fee plus pay-per-clicks to write content. If you're an expert in a field, you could make some good money doing this.

Write Top Lists. If you're good at coming up with lists, some websites, one being Listverse, will pay you $100 to write a compelling "Top 10" list. If you're full of great ideas you could easily make a couple hundred dollars.

Be a Review Writer. Some companies will pay you to review anything from music to products. Usually they will send you a free sample to try and then pay you to write an honest review. Check out websites such as ExpoTV, SponseredReviews, or Slicethepie.com.

Freelance Work and Side Gigs

oDesk. oDesk is a leading freelancer's website where you can sign up and apply to gigs for anything from web and software development, networking and information systems, creative writing, virtual assistant work, art design, business services, customer service and sales/marketing. The jobs on this website range from low-paying beginner's jobs to more paid, highly advanced jobs. It's a great place to start if you want to make extra money doing freelance work on the side.

Elance. Elance is very similar to oDesk in the way it works and the job categories, except freelancers can additionally find legal, engineering, and manufacturing gigs.

Here are some great tips on how to be successful on oDesk and Elance:

- Upload a professional-looking photo of yourself. The more professional, the better, because it can help reflect your solid work ethic. Also, people like to do business with others to whom they can match a face to a name. Finally, it helps verify the legitimacy of your profile.

- Sell yourself. If you're a writer, add some of your writing samples to your portfolio. If you're an artist, upload some of your best drawings. The better you can sell yourself, the more likely you are to win a bid for a job. No past project is too small to display!

- Write a killer cover letter. To apply to gigs on oDesk and Elance, you must send the client a cover letter, explaining why you'd be a good fit for the job. Make the cover letter short, simple, and to the point. Let the client know what value you can bring to them and any experience you have that could help you do the job better.

- Finally, when you're awarded a contract, do the best job possible. Clients can leave you feedback, which can boost or lower your chances of getting another job, depending on how well they think you did.

Craigslist. If you're a freelancer, you can sometimes get lucky on Craigslist. Depending on your area, you can often find lots of great working opportunities, one-time manual labor gigs, technology opportunities, and miscellaneous ways to make extra money. Often times, people will put ads up for one-time jobs. For example, somebody in your area might be looking to pay another person in the area to help them move some furniture. You can also sell used items there.

Here are some helpful tips on how to be successful at making making on Craigslist:

- Keep an eye out for local jobs, that require little or no travel. If you see a job for helping to move a couch but it's 50 miles away form where you live, it probably wouldn't be worth it as much as if it were just on the other side of town.

- Be wary of scams. Although Craigslist is a great website, it is often loaded with scams. If you go somewhere to do a job, always let somebody know where you're going. Never give out personal information to anybody you do not know or do not feel comfortable with.

Ebay. Ebay is a great place to sell your old stuff for some extra money. The trick for making a profit on eBay is to research the item that you are selling. Check out what it's going for on eBay as well as other online retail sites such as Amazon. For the best results, only list products that are useful and, if possible, in high demand. As an added benefit, you'll reduce the clutter in your home and that can help you stay less stressed.

Amazon. Amazon is a great online retail site and there are several ways to make money using it. Like eBay, you can resell products that you no longer need. With

Amazon, you can list "used" versions of an item for sale against "new" versions, as many people will opt for used items that are in good condition. Writers can write and sell e-books on the site. Amazon also hosts an affiliate program, where you can make a commission when you refer another person to a product being sold on their website.

Surveys. Surveys are one of the most commonly known ways to make extra money from home. Though it is not as "easy" as it sounds and there are many scam survey sites that promise you lots of money in exchange for your opinion, there still are some legitimate websites out there that you can use. Some of the best legitimate survey websites are Opinion Outpost, Survey Spot, Valued Opinions, and InboxDollars. While the truth is that taking surveys online probably *won't* net you a huge amount of money, it is possible to make at least $100 a month if you're truly dedicated.

Here are some great tips for being successful with surveys:

- Set up a separate email account for survey websites. Some survey websites will pay you a couple of cents just to open and read emails and if you use your personal email address, your inbox can get really jammed up. Having a separate account can help you manage your surveys better.

- Look out for scams—usual scam signs include websites with no company information, no privacy policy, sites that immediately ask you only for your first and last name plus email address, and sites with offers that sound too good to be true (i.e., get paid $50 to take a 5 minute survey).

- Some surveys are very specific and you will have to take a short questionnaire to see if you qualify. So if you see an offer to take a survey about movies but you've only gone to the movies once in the past 10 years, you probably won't qualify. Try to pick surveys that you think will best suit you.

- Some surveys are based on specific demographics, so if the survey is looking for opinions from African American males and you're an Asian woman, you will probably get disqualified. Try to see if there are any certain requirements to taking a survey before trying to fill it out.

- Most legitimate surveys know whether you're rushing through the questions and/or not paying attention. If you fly through a survey, most likely the computer will pick it up and you will not get paid. Answer all questions honestly, thoroughly, and consistently or else you may end up wasting a good 10-20 minutes of your time.

Etsy. If your talent niche is arts and crafts, Etsy is a great website to use for selling your creations. On Etsy, many people sell hand-crafted mugs, jewelry, customized artwork and much more. If you're an artist, consider creating your own Esty shop to start building a customer base and making a nice little side income.

Here are some great tips on how to be successful on Etsy:

- Treat it as a real business. Have a plan for business development and marketing. You can always just post your items and hope that they will sell, but marketing them can greatly boost your chances of a nice profit.

- For every product you sell, make sure you take at least 3-5 pictures of it from different angles. Shoppers will like to see a product from several different angles, especially when buying online. If they can't see what they're buying, why would they want to spend their money on it?
- Like eBay, research similar products to see what price they're going for. If you overprice yourself, you may sell nothing at all.

- Be Patient. Your products probably won't sell the minute you post them. Focus on marketing them and perform great customer service to increase the chances of paying clients referring new clients to you.

Flipping Domain Names. Flipping domain names is a really cool way to make money on the side. The idea of flipping domain names is to purchase expired or unregistered domain names and resell them for a profit. There are many ways to obtain domain names to sell later. You can purchase new ones yourself at places like GoDaddy and then sell them for a higher price later on. You can also sell domain names in online forums. Another popular way to buy domain names is to use Namejet, which is an online auction website where you can place bids on domain names that are either dead, expired, or unwanted and then resell for a profit.

Here are some great tips on how to be successful at flipping domain names:

- Do your research! Only bid on domain names that you think will sell well. Use Google to see what is trending and then look for websites whose domains could use an upgrade. Then offer to sell the domain to the owner of that website.

- Stay motivated and inspirational. Tell yourself that if you bought a domain for $1,000, you'll try to flip it at $2,000 to get double the profit. Domain flipping can be a very tricky process so it is important not to underprice yourself.

- As always, remember to try and bring value to the person you're trying to sell the domain too. For example, do some research and tell them how much more traffic they could get with a more professional domain name.

If you can show a buyer what your product will do for them, he or she will be more likely to make the purchase.

Passive Income

Building passive income is a great way to earn extra money on the side and it rolls in when you're sleeping—literally! Specifically, passive income is an automated system that enables you to earn cash flow, make transactions, and grow your income without having to be consciously present. The best thing about passive income is that it doesn't interfere with your time—and remember, time is precious and limited.

The market for digital goods is really great for generating passive income. A great entrepreneur once told me that the best way to make more money is to create something once and then sell it over and over again. What better way than to sell digital goods (ebooks, stock images, music, videos, courses, etc). All you have to do is create something, sell it as downloadable content (eliminating shipping and packing procedures), and let the money roll in. Of course, it can be much more difficult than that, especially at the beginning, but after all the hard work is done, it is very satisfying to sit back and reap the rewards months or even years later. Here are some great ideas on how to generate passive income:

Write Ebooks. Are you an expert in your field? Do you have a talent for writing fiction? If your writing skills are good and you think you have something to share with the world of readers, put it in an ebook and let people buy it. There are many great platforms available online in which you can upload your ebook for free and charge people money to read it. Some of the best platforms I've seen are Kindle Direct Publishing and Smashwords among others. The commission that you make off your book after the hosting site takes its slice may not be very big, but if you write a best-seller and it goes viral, you could easily generate some great income.

Keep a Blog. Keeping a blog is another great way to generate passive income. The key here is to hire a ghostwriter to write your blog for you, otherwise it wouldn't really be passive. The best idea is to a write a blog that focuses around one specific topic. When you're writing about a specific niche, you can sign up for an affiliate program to help sell related products and make even more money. When setting up a blog to generate passive income, you will need to outsource work and hire people to help you write content, set up search-engine optimization, do marketing, etc, but you can usually find this kind of help for fairly cheap online.

Youtube Monetization. If you're really talented with films and video editing, YouTube might be a good source of side income for you. If you're a creator of original, unique videos that get many views a day, you may be eligible to monetize your YouTube account, meaning that you can get paid based on how many viewers come to your page, watch your videos, and click on the ads that pop up on the videos.

Here are some great tips on being successful with YouTube Monetization:

- Make quality videos only. Nobody wants to watch a video that is fuzzy, poorly lit, and/or that has scratchy audio. Videos of poor quality will most likely not generate any views.

- Never upload content that is not yours. If you incur a copyright claim and you lose, your account could end up getting suspended and you may be in violation of the law.

- Properly tag your video with related search-terms to generate more clicks and views.

- How-To videos are the best kind to make if you want to generate a lot of views. Often times, people like to have a visual guide of doing something they've never done before. For example, not everyone knows how to change a headlight, but it's simple enough to do if they had a step-by-step video. How many people are in need of replacing a burned out headlight? Try to think that way—what is a problem that many people need a solution too? Can I provide good direction? If you can master really good How-To videos, you'll most likely be successful.

Sell Your Photography. Are you one of those people who just take amazing photos, even ones that you take on your cell phone camera? Stock photography is an easy way to generate passive income because all you need to do is take one amazing picture and then let people around the world use it for their content. The market for stock photography is good because people like to use pictures in all sorts of digital mediums and they will pay top dollar for the best ones. Some great websites to start out selling your stock photography on are Alamy, Shutterstock, Dreamstime, and iStockPhoto.

Sell Your Music. If you have a musical talent, what better way to use it than to sell your music to others for their listening pleasure? Perform once, sell always. Apple iTunes allows users to apply to have their music sold on the platform. The website TuneCore is also a great resource for distributing paid music.

The fun part about passive income is that it presents you the challenge of trying to "get big." The more people who are exposed to your content, the more money you can make. Generating good money from passive income is almost like high-end gambling—you never know whether your content will go viral or not, but either way, you're still going to make money.

Chapter 5: Developing Your Money-Making Ideas

You just learned about some great money making ideas and various ways to get started making money. However, don't think that your options are limited—in fact, your money-making ideas are unlimited, especially if you can create a breakthrough product, service, or idea. Everybody's minds work differently, so it would be impossible to list every single great money-making idea in the world here. However, you *can* learn how to develop your ideas so that whenever something comes to your mind, you can get up and take action.

Keep Your Ideas Together. If an amazing idea comes to your mind but you don't have the time and/or resources to work on it yet, write it down and keep all of your ideas together. You can keep an idea notebook or even write them down on slips of paper and keep them in a box. Don't hesitate to write your ideas down because they can become easily forgotten *and* by writing them down, you pose a higher chance of taking action on them. If writing them down is your thing, a digital voice recorder can come in very handy. You can quickly record any idea you may have and then store all those ideas in a prominent place on your computer that you can easily listen to at your convenience.

Be Knowledgeable. Although it may seem like it, most ideas don't just appear out of nowhere. Often times, they're derived from something that already exists. People who have a talent for taking a new angle on something old would probably agree. Do what you can to stay knowledgeable and up to date on current events for the best chance of coming up with an idea.

Think. Sometimes a great idea can come from simply connecting the dots between two things. Have an open mind and don't be afraid to think. When you open your mind up, it can be much easier to make a genius realization. Be creative and use your imagination to your advantage. Ask yourself, "what if" questions. Another great way for coming up with ideas is to try and finish this sentence: "There has got to be a better way to..."

Test Out Your Idea. If applicable, test out your idea before you put it into action. This can be as simple as gathering up a handful of clients for a soft-sell or going out into the real world and using your observational skills to confirm your theories and ideas. By testing out your idea before you take action on it, you can potentially save yourself a lot of time and trouble if you find the idea might not work as well as you imagined.

Watch Your Timing. Timing can make or break your idea. Take for example the Power Glove for the original Nintendo Entertainment System, which came out in the 1980's. The concept of the Power Glove was that the player could put the glove, which had a built-in controller/computer, on their hand and control the game by the movement of their hand, arm, and fingers. The product failed miserably and the technology worked poorly. However, Nintendo rolled out the Wii gaming console in the late 2000's which came with technology that allows players to control the game wirelessly with a motion-censored controller. It's pretty much the same concept of the Power Glove, just without the glove. The Wii was a huge success and is now Nintendo's main gaming system. So they had the idea in the 80's, but had to wait until the technology was better to fully implement it for mass success.

Is Your Idea Helpful? All in all, ask yourself if your idea will help people. If it doesn't help people in any way, it probably will not be as profitable as you had hoped. Consumers buy things to solve problems more than they buy things just for fun.

In conclusion, no matter what your idea is, know that you *can* develop it into something great. Use this checklist to make sure that your idea is awesome from the start:

- Would my idea solve a real problem among people?
- How can I develop my idea to make it a solution?
- Am I passionate about my idea?
- Is my idea testable?
- Is the world ready for my idea right now or would it be better to wait?

Chapter 6: Investing

Investing is a broad yet amazing topic. The best part about investing is that your money goes out and works for you instead of the other way around. Being an investor is pretty much as far as you can go to make your money work for you. It often requires minimal work—just lots of knowledge, a high-tolerance for risk taking, and the willpower and determination to see it through. This chapter will take a look at some of the most common ways to get started with investing.

Invest in Your Business

If you have a business, there are many great ways to make investments that you can make you more money in the future. One of the most common forms of business investing is to invest in a start-up business. If you decide to just wake up one day and start a business without putting any money toward planning, research, marketing, etc, you probably won't be in business very long and you probably won't make any money. That being said, if you take out a $10,000 business loan and put it toward writing a business plan, marketing your services, hiring a qualified employee, etc, you are investing in your business. The money you invest into it can help you get started on the right foot. So, if you invest $10,000 into your business and you make $5,000 a year, your investment will be paid off in about two years and after that, the $5,000 each year goes right into your pocket!

Another form of a smart business investment is to invest in yourself. When you are self-employed and a sole proprietor of a business, your business stops making money when you stop working. If you want to be an expert in your field and charge clients more money for your work, you can probably get away with working fewer hours. If you're just starting out, you will have to charge your clients a rate that reflects your experience. So, if you're a freelance writer and you're just starting out and you have no credentials, you'll probably have to make do with lots of low-paying jobs until you have built up your reputation. However, you can invest in further education, reading books to strengthen your skills, or you just invest so much time in your area of work that your experience naturally goes up. Over time, you can charge higher and higher rates.

Make Your Money Work For You

Another type of investment is to make your money go out and work for you. One common way people do this is that they lend out their money and charge people interest. You can easily do this through a bank or through a private agreement.

Here is a great example: Say you lend somebody $150,000 to buy a house because they have bad credit. If you charge them a 13% interest rate on that $150,000 loan, you'll be able to make $1,625 a month just on interest alone.

Invest in Property

By investing in property, usually for business purposes, you can make a great profit after the investment is paid off. For example, if you buy a car for $25,000 and use it as a taxi cab, you can pay the investment off in 5 years if you bring in $5,000 a year. Then, after 5 years, you can make a profit for as long as you operate the cab. If you buy a home for $100,000 and rent it out at $2,000 a month, you can make your money back in roughly 4 and half years. After that, you make a $24,000 profit every year provided that you rent out the house consistently.

To be really successful in real estate investing while avoiding the hard work of buying run-down homes and spending time fixing them up, you can network with real estate professionals and make some friends who are constantly looking to sell property. Then, network with those who are looking to buy property. Once you do that, you can collect a finder's fee. For example, if you know somebody who is selling a run-down property for $15,000 and you know somebody who is looking to buy a property within the $20,000 range, bring the buyer and seller together and ask the seller to give you a commission for bringing him a sale.

Invest in Other Businesses

If you make an investment in another business, you essentially get a cut of the money back. For example, if you make a 50% investment in a skateboard shop and the shop makes $10,000 after expenses, you will receive $5,000 of that money. For some great, professional tips on investing in other businesses, be sure to check out these great visual tutorials:

Bill Ackman: Invest in the Business You Can Own Forever

Warren Buffet: How Do You Decide What to Invest Your Time and Money In?

Business Financing: How To Invest in a Start-Up Business

Capital Gain Incomes

This type of investing is probably the simplest. A capital gain income is when you go out and buy something at one price and then turn around and sell it for a higher price. The difference between the price you bought it at and the price you sold it at is your capital gain. A great business coach once gave me a secret about being successful with money: he said that when you start a business, do not get emotionally attached to it, but rather get it up to par and sell it for more than it cost to start it. That way, the more businesses you can establish and sell, the more capital gains you can make.

Invest in Stocks

Investing in stocks is another great method of investment, especially for those who love to take risks. When you purchase a stock it means you now own a share of a certain company. There are two different types of stock—preferred and common. Preferred stock is best for those who don't get excited by risk taking because the price of the stock doesn't tend to fluctuate. Preferred stock also pays dividends to shareholders. That means that holders of preferred stock have a claim to a company if it goes bankrupt over common stock holders. Common stock is more risky but its return potential is much higher.

To make money with stocks, you have to pay attention to supply and demand. When you own a share of a company and that company does well, more people will want to buy into it. As with supply and demand, the price of the stock will go up as more people want it. If you choose to sell that stock when the demand goes up, you'll make a profit. Another way to make money from owning stocks is to get paid with a dividend. Some companies will pay shareholders a small dividend every quarter.

Here are some great visual resources that you can use for more information on investing in stocks:

Stock Market For Beginners – Advice by Warren Buffet

Warren Buffet: How Should the Average Person Invest in the Stock Market?

Invest in Bonds

A bond is where investors lend money to businesses and organizations as well as the government when the loan they need is too big to get from a bank. By investing in bonds, the organization that sells bonds (the bond issuer) will charge the buyer an interest rate. By lending out your personal money you will be able to collect that interest rate over a certain period of time. Bondholders have first priority when bankruptcy hits and are much less riskier than investing in stocks.

Here are some great visual resources that you can use for more information on investing in bonds:

How Bond Investing Works

The Basics of Bonds

Conclusion

I hope this book was able to help you to realize all the different things that you can do to help improve your own personal financial situation!

The next step is to start by going back to Chapter 1 and doing the special exercises, if you haven't already. Now that you have an overview of what you can do to earn and save money, go back and really spend some time on the other exercises. Once completed, you can start implementing your favorite ideas and strategies that you feel will give you the greatest success. Remember to start out with a great attitude and the belief that you deserve great financial success! Be sure to keep your motivations for financial success firmly in your mind and proceed with confidence knowing that you will not give up and that you're destined to succeed!

Finally, if you discovered at least one thing that has helped you or that you think would be beneficial to someone else, be sure to take a few seconds to easily post a quick positive review. As an author, your positive feedback is desperately needed. Your highly valuable five star reviews are like a river of golden joy flowing through a sunny forest of mighty trees and beautiful flowers! *To do your good deed in making the world a better place by helping others with your valuable insight, just leave a nice review.*

Thanks and Best of Luck

My Other Books and Audio Books
www.AcesEbooks.com

Business & Finance Books

LEADERSHIP

THE TOP 100 BEST WAYS TO BE A GREAT LEADER

Ace McCloud

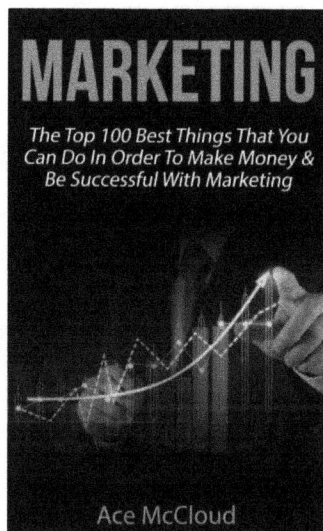

MARKETING

The Top 100 Best Things That You Can Do In Order To Make Money & Be Successful With Marketing

Ace McCloud

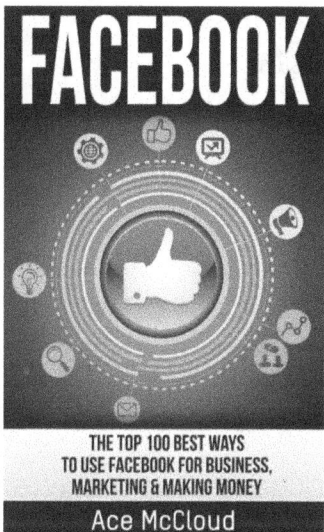

FACEBOOK

THE TOP 100 BEST WAYS TO USE FACEBOOK FOR BUSINESS, MARKETING & MAKING MONEY

Ace McCloud

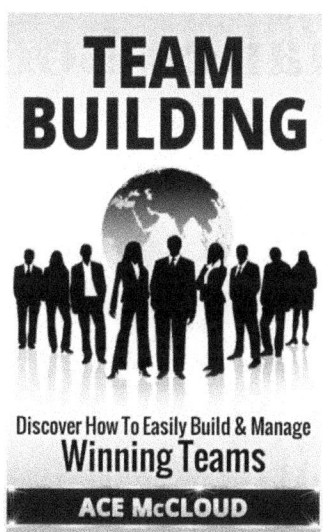

TEAM BUILDING

Discover How To Easily Build & Manage **Winning Teams**

ACE McCLOUD

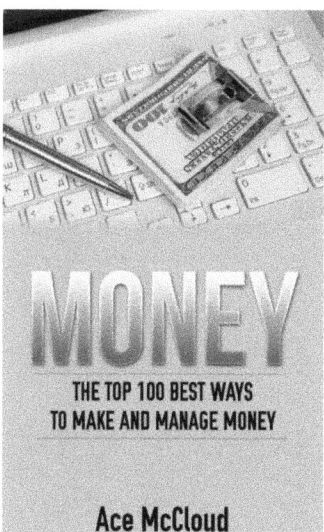

MONEY

THE TOP 100 BEST WAYS TO MAKE AND MANAGE MONEY

Ace McCloud

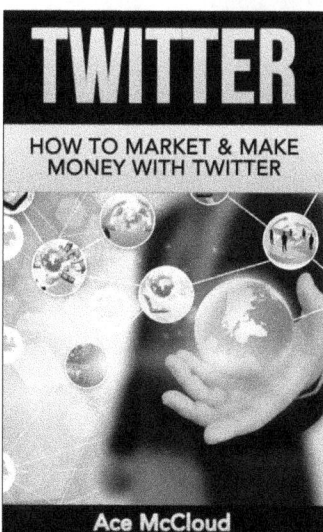

TWITTER

HOW TO MARKET & MAKE MONEY WITH TWITTER

Ace McCloud

COMMUNICATION SKILLS

Discover The Best Ways To Communicate,
Be Charismatic, Use Body Language,
Persuade & Be A Great Conversationalist

Ace McCloud

YouTube

THE TOP 100 BEST WAYS
TO MARKET & MAKE MONEY WITH YOUTUBE

Ace McCloud

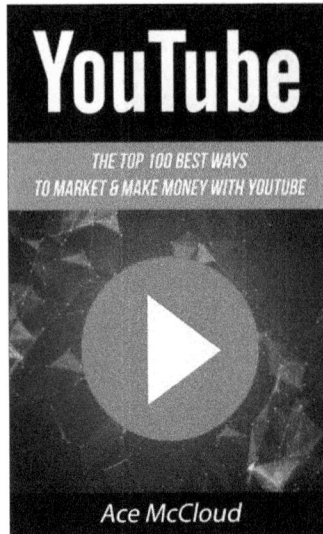

Peak Performance Books

SUCCESS

SUCCESS STRATEGIES

THE TOP 100 BEST WAYS TO BE SUCCESSFUL

Ace McCloud

Ace McCloud

HABIT

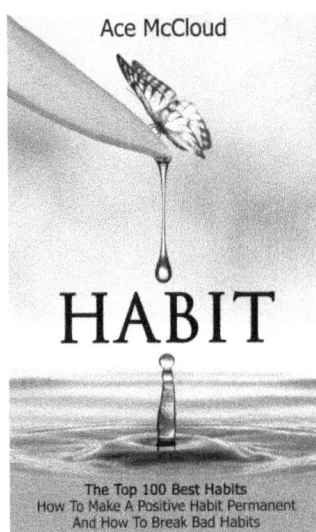

The Top 100 Best Habits
How To Make A Positive Habit Permanent
And How To Break Bad Habits

MOTIVATION

MASTER THE POWER OF MOTIVATION
TO PROPEL YOURSELF TO SUCCESS

Ace McCloud

ATTITUDE

Discover The True Power Of
A Positive Attitude

Ace McCloud

SELF DISCIPLINE

Unleash The Power Of Self Discipline,
Influence And Willpower In Your Life
To Achieve Anything

Ace McCloud

Competitive Strategies

WINNING STRATEGIES

The Top 100 Best Strategies
For Peak Performance During Competitions

Ace McCloud

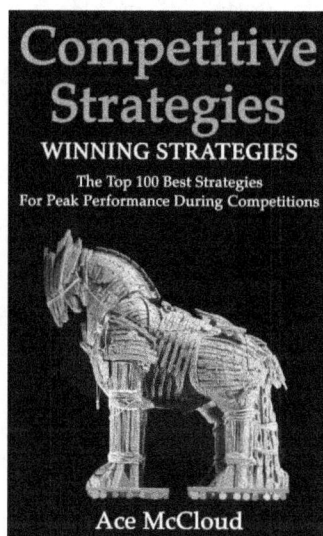

Be sure to check out my audio books as well!

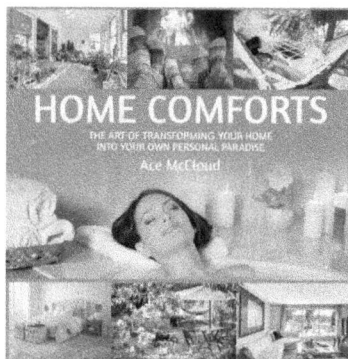

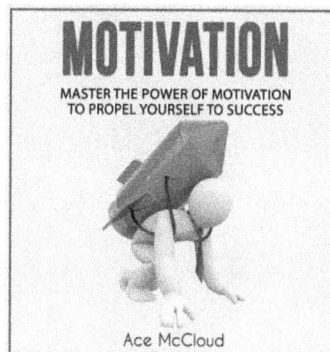

Happiness

The Top 100 Best Ways
To Feel Good & Be Happy

Ace McCloud

HOME COMFORTS

THE ART OF TRANSFORMING YOUR HOME
INTO YOUR OWN PERSONAL PARADISE

Ace McCloud

MOTIVATION

MASTER THE POWER OF MOTIVATION
TO PROPEL YOURSELF TO SUCCESS

Ace McCloud

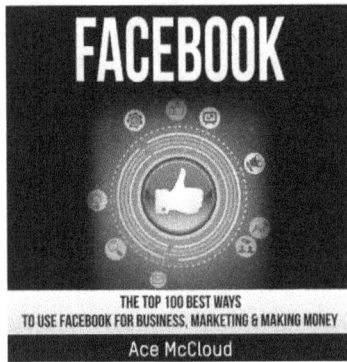

FACEBOOK

THE TOP 100 BEST WAYS
TO USE FACEBOOK FOR BUSINESS, MARKETING & MAKING MONEY

Ace McCloud

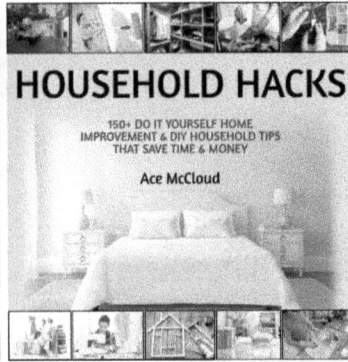

HOUSEHOLD HACKS

150+ DO IT YOURSELF HOME
IMPROVEMENT & DIY HOUSEHOLD TIPS
THAT SAVE TIME & MONEY

Ace McCloud

SUCCESS
SUCCESS STRATEGIES

THE TOP 100 BEST WAYS TO BE SUCCESSFUL

Ace McCloud

Check out my website at: **www.AcesEbooks.com** for a complete list of all of my books and high quality audio books. I enjoy bringing you the best knowledge in the world and wish you the best in using this information to make your journey through life better and more enjoyable! **Best of luck to you!**